Praise for OMG!...

"As the mother of two daughters and advocate for women, I applaud Skylarr Marsh for *OMG! Operating as a Millennial with God*. She crafted the perfect book to encourage, empower and inspire young ladies to live their best."
—Karen M.R. Townsend, PhD, CEO of KTownsend Consulting
DrKarenTownsend.com

"Skylarr poured her heart into an engaging and relevant inspirational book. It provides spiritual clarity to overcome life's challenges and develop a closer relationship with God. Her messages align with Scripture to help catapult a reader's spirit. *OMG!* delivers!"
—LaTonya Branham, PhD, author and educator
LaTonyaBranham.com

"This book is a valuable tool to help millennials reflect on who they are and how God sees them. Skylarr digs deep into real issues and explains how to apply the Word to life's challenges. *OMG!* gives hope and authority to youth who thought they were alone and powerless."
—Phillitia Charlton, author and personal development coach
CharltonCharlton.com

"*OMG! Operating as a Millennial with God* is a spiritual guide to help live a healthier lifestyle. I love the supportive biblical context throughout the chapters. The content is full of transparency and the language is simple, yet powerful. This book is helpful for anyone attempting to overcome obstacles while pursuing their dreams."

—Bobbie Watkins, author of *A Search for HER New Beginning* and CEO of Obedience Ink ObedienceInk.com

OMG!
Operating as a Millennial with God

Skylarr-Nicole Marsh

Published by
Queen V Publishing
Dayton, OH
QueenVPublishing.com

Published by
Queen V Publishing
Dayton, OH
QueenVPublishing.com

Copyright © 2019 by Skylarr-Nicole Marsh

All rights reserved. No part of this book may be reproduced or transmitted in any form or by any means, electronic or mechanical, without prior written consent of the author, except for the inclusion of brief quotes in a review.

Unless otherwise noted, Scriptures are from the Amplified Version of the Holy Bible.

Library of Congress Control Number: 2019937984

ISBN-13: 978-0-9962991-2-1

Cover design by CandaceK

Edited by Valerie J. Lewis Coleman of Pen of the Writer PenOfTheWriter.com

Printed in the United States of America

Dedication

To my father, Ritchie Marsh:
I wish you were here. I know you would be proud of me. Although I don't understand God's reason for taking you, know that I appreciate you and everything you taught me. Thank you for being an amazing father. Forever in my heart,
Skylarr

Table of Contents

Foreword 9
Introduction 11
In Your Strength 13

    Depression 15
    Discouraged 19
    Fear 23
    Feeling Unloved 27
    Life Losses 31
    Losing Friends 35
    Struggles in School 39
    Struggling to Pray 43

In Christ 47

    God Wants You, Not Your Plans 49
    The Promises of God 53
    God's Strength 57
    God's Timing 61
    Forgiveness 65
    Calling on Jesus 71
    The Beauty in Being You 75
    A Better Relationship with God 79
    Finding Your Identity in Christ 83
    Speak God's Word over Your Life 87
    Living for Christ 93
    Faith 97

Trusting God	101
Pursuing Peace	105
Spiritual Reference	109
The Holy Spirit	111
Acknowledgements	115
About the Author	117
About Queen V Publishing	119

Foreword

Having been Skylarr's "cheerleader" for a number of years, I am overjoyed and honored to be part of her amazing endeavor.

Skylarr has always been a quality young lady. She was thirteen years old when I taught her mother's Sunday School class. She is the product of Christian parents who taught her the value of living a life pleasing to God and family. Because she walks the walk she talks, her life is a model for young people to emulate.

Skylarr's contagious personality, love of life and concern for people make her an asset to the community and the world. Paraphrasing Proverbs 18:24, to have a friend, you must first be friendly. Skylarr is the ultimate friend. Her motives are pure and genuine. She is trustworthy and reliable. She encourages and supports.

This book is a must-read for any millennial seeking a deeper relationship with Christ! SUCCESS follows Skylarr and awaits YOU!

Proud to be a friend,
Clinton E. Yokley, deacon, teacher and ministry leader

Skylarr-Nicole Marsh

Introduction

My life is nowhere near perfect. I have experienced great loss, betrayal and disappointments. It wasn't until I developed an intimate relationship with God that I realized He is responsible for me, and He wants only the best for me.

I am grateful that God placed this book on my heart. The process wasn't easy, but He inspired each lesson as a personal message to you.

My prayer is that *OMG! Operating as a Millennial with God* encourages you with an understanding of who you are, and who God is to you. Be transparent about your relationship with Him, your prayer life and your feelings. Depression, school troubles and feeling inadequate can blind you from seeing yourself the way God sees you: victorious, fearfully and wonderfully made and loved without condition.

With God's help, you can get through anything. I pray you grow closer to Him; He blesses you beyond your expectations and you go to Him first for every need.

Sincerely,
Skylarr-Nicole R. Marsh

"God is going to work it all out for the good. All the pain, frustration, heartbreak; somehow, and in some way. He is going to use all of the broken pieces to make a beautiful masterpiece."
— Ashley Hetherington

In Your Strength

"God has a reason for allowing things to happen. We may never understand His wisdom, but we simply have to trust His will."
— BibleQuote365.com

OMG! *Operating as a Millennial with God*

Depression

When you feel like life is too much to handle, you can easily slip into emptiness, which can lead to depression. I'm not a therapist, but I encourage you to take your problems to God.

When the righteous cry [for help], the Lord hears and rescues them from all their distress and troubles. The Lord is near to the heartbroken, and He saves those who are crushed in spirit (contrite in heart, truly sorry for their sin).
—Psalm 34:17-18

Although the enemy will launch (form) attacks (weapons), walk by faith, not by sight. God promised that you will win against the spirit of depression, if you seek His face and invite Him to intervene in your earthly matter. God will hear you and put a new song in your heart. Cast all your cares on Him. Why? Because He cares for you.

Answer me quickly, O Lord, my spirit fails; Do not hide Your face from me, or I will become like those who go down into the pit (grave). Let me hear Your lovingkindness in the morning, for I trust in You. Teach me the way in which I should walk, for I lift up my soul to You.
—Psalm 143:7-8

I waited patiently and expectantly for the Lord; and He inclined to me and heard my cry. He brought me up out of a horrible pit [of tumult and of destruction], out of the miry clay, and He set my feet upon a rock, steadying my footsteps and establishing my path. He put a new song in my mouth, a song of praise to our God; many will see and fear [with great reverence], and will trust confidently in the Lord.
—Psalm 40:1-3

"No weapon formed against you shall prosper, and every tongue which rises against you in judgment You shall condemn. This is the heritage of the servants of the Lord, and their righteousness is from Me," says the Lord.
—Isaiah 54:17 NJKV

When you read the Bible, personalize God's Word by replacing the blanks with your name or pronoun "me" as follows:

"No weapon formed against _____ shall prosper, and every tongue which rises against _____ in judgment You shall condemn. This is the heritage of the servants of the Lord, and their righteousness is from Me," says the Lord.

These things I have spoken to you, that in Me you may have peace. In the world you will have

OMG! Operating as a Millennial with God

tribulation; but be of good cheer, I have overcome the world.
—John 16:33 NKJV

Blessed [gratefully praised and adored] be the God and Father of our Lord Jesus Christ, the Father of mercies and the God of all comfort, who comforts and encourages us in every trouble so that we will be able to comfort and encourage those who are in any kind of trouble, with the comfort with which we ourselves are comforted by God.
—2 Corinthians 1:3-4

Dear God, I feel less than what You have created me to be. Depression, doubt, stress and anger are not Your desire for me. I humbly ask for Your help. I know that You will hear me, lift me and establish me. Thank You for sending Your Word to help overcome depression. In Jesus' name, amen.

—Fight depression with God's Word.
He cares for you—

Reflection Questions

Awareness is the first step to healing. What does depression look like for you?

_____

_____

_____

What things can/do you do to encourage yourself?

_____

_____

_____

When you feel depressed, what Scriptures make you joyful?

_____

_____

_____

_____

_____

_____

_____

Discouraged

If you're not careful, life situations can discourage you. Family, friends or not passing a test can be frustrating. At some point, everyone feels discouraged, but it's good to know that you can go to God with every issue. In moments of weakness, God will encourage you through reading His Word, prayer or sending someone with godly advice. Not everything happens the way you plan, and your timing is not God's timing. He has only one plan for you and it does not include failure. God sees your hurt, disappointments and tears. His sovereign hand realigns you and His plan is on schedule. Be encouraged.

Do not fear [anything], for I am with you; do not be afraid, for I am your God. I will strengthen you, be assured I will help you; I will certainly take hold of you with My righteous right hand [a hand of justice, of power, of victory, of salvation].
—Isaiah 41:10

Be strong and courageous, do not be afraid or tremble in dread before them, for it is the Lord your God who goes with you. He will not fail you or abandon you.
–Deuteronomy 31:6

He only is my rock and my salvation; My fortress and my defense, I will not be shaken or discouraged.
—Psalm 62:6

Dear God, thank You for encouraging me when I feel defeated. Your Word gives voice to every season, circumstance and emotion I experience. When I feel discouraged, I know that You are strong within me. I won't be defeated because of Your strength and loving kindness. In Jesus' name, amen.

—Disappointments come to make you stronger—

OMG! Operating as a Millennial with God

Reflection Questions

Do you trust God and His plan for you while discouraged?

_____

_____

_____

Your ways aren't God's ways, so how do you plan to shift your perspective concerning your problems?

_____

_____

_____

When you feel discouraged, what Scriptures encourage you?

_____

_____

_____

_____

_____

_____

"Your struggle will transform into your testimony."
—Tatiana Jerome

OMG! Operating as a Millennial with God

Fear

According to *Webster's Dictionary*, fear is "an unpleasant emotion caused by the belief that someone or something is dangerous, likely to cause pain, or a threat."

Is doing what God told you to do scary? Do you fear being who He called you to be? Do you fear utilizing the gifts He placed in you? Do you fear His plans for you? Fear limits you from reaching your God-given potential. You have freedom from fear because God gave you a sound mind, sure foundation and strong promises. When you entrust your life to Him, you have no reason to fear.

I sought the Lord [on the authority of His Word], and He answered me, and delivered me from all my fears.
—Psalm 34:4

Say to those with an anxious and panic-stricken heart, "Be strong, fear not! Indeed, your God will come with vengeance [for the ungodly]; the retribution of God will come, but He will save you."
—Isaiah 35:4

For God did not give us a spirit of timidity or cowardice or fear, but [He has given us a spirit] of

power and of love and of sound judgment and personal discipline [abilities that result in a calm, well-balanced mind and self-control].
—2 Timothy 1:7

Dear God, Your Word says that You did not give us the spirit of fear. When I feel anxiety and worry rising in me, help me recall that You are in control. Thank You for giving me a peaceful spirit to trust You; even when I should be afraid. In Jesus' name, amen.

—Relax. Don't fear. God's got it!—

Reflections of My Heart

Fear held me back from things I wanted to do, and things that God told me to do. I am ready to experience the freedom of the Lord. Even when I'm afraid, my purpose and God's plan have to go forth. I am free from the fear of my future. I am free from thinking my talents and gifts are not good enough. I am free of my fear to drive. I am stepping out on faith to live my dreams, and the abundant life God has for me. I bind fear and loose confidence. Jesus already won, so fear is not allowed to occupy space in my head or heart. I thank God for a calm mind and peaceful spirit.

OMG! Operating as a Millennial with God

Reflection Questions

What do you fear?

_____

_____

_____

How has that fear—whether real or imagined—affected you?

_____

_____

_____

What Scriptures calm you when you feel afraid?

_____

_____

_____

_____

_____

_____

_____

_____

"Fear may rise up, but faith always wins."
— Tiffany Parry

OMG! Operating as a Millennial with God

Feeling Unloved

Have you ever felt like no one likes, loves or appreciates you? Although you may feel that way, those feelings are tricks of the enemy. When you "get in your feelings," you tend to feel—and ultimately believe—things that aren't true. I have lived that situation plenty of times. The love the world gives is temporary and based on what someone can get from you. The love of God surpasses everything because it is pure and selfless. He wants peace, joy and happiness for you. According to Romans 8:31-39, your fears, bitterness and failed relationships cannot separate you from His unconditional love.

The Lord appeared to me from ages past, saying, "I have loved you with an everlasting love; Therefore with loving kindness I have drawn you and continued My faithfulness to you."
—Jeremiah 31:3

Speak this Scripture replacing the blanks with your name:
"I have loved _____ with an everlasting love; Therefore with loving kindness I have drawn _____ and continued My faithfulness to _____."

God, thank You for showing me true love. Thank You for the ability to love myself—and others—the way You love me. Thank You for sending Your Word when I feel like I'm unlovable. Thank You for sending Your Son as the perfect example of how love is supposed to look. I am enough through You. In Jesus' name, amen.

—Love yourself and others with the love of Christ—

OMG! Operating as a Millennial with God

Reflection Questions

What situations make you feel like you are not loved?

_____

_____

_____

How do you work through that feeling?

_____

_____

_____

When you feel unloved, what Scriptures affirm that He loves you?

_____

_____

_____

_____

_____

_____

_____

_____

"Though we are incomplete, God loves us completely. Though we are imperfect, He loves us perfectly. Though we may feel lost and without compass, God's love encompasses us completely."
—Deiter F. Uchtdorf

Life Losses

Life comes with ups-and-downs and wins-and-losses including losing a job, loved ones, money or your health. The biblical story of Job is the perfect example of loss. Job had a family, land and lots of money. He was upright before the Lord with a hedge of protection around him. Satan asked for permission to attack Job and God granted it. Why? Because He knew Job was faithful. He knew that Job loved Him wholeheartedly. So even when Job lost everything and felt like God was angry with him, he never let go of his faith as noted below:

> *And said, "Naked came I out of my mother's womb, and naked shall I return thither: the Lord gave, and the Lord hath taken away; blessed be the name of the Lord."*
> —Job 1:21 KJV

> *Though He slay me, yet will I trust in Him: but I will maintain mine own ways before Him.*
> —Job 13:15 KJV

Although you may feel like God has forgotten you, know that your losses, heartbreaks and pain are designed to bring you closer to Him. Anger and bitterness will not change the situation, so submit your way to His. God called you into repentance, and

His ways are just. As promised in His Word, He will bless and restore you. Because of his faithfulness, Job received double for his trouble. God blessed him with more children, more land and more wealth. He gives; He takes; He's Sovereign.

> *For I know that my Redeemer and Vindicator lives, and at the last He will take His stand upon the earth.*
> —Job 19:25

> *And we know [with great confidence] that God [who is deeply concerned about us] causes all things to work together [as a plan] for good for those who love God, to those who are called according to His plan and purpose.*
> —Romans 8:28

God, help me understand that despite loss, I am not lost in You. You allow obstacles to prove my love for You, but Satan cannot do anything to me without Your permission. Father, what do You want me to learn in this situation? I trust Your plans for me and wait for complete restoration. In Jesus' name, amen.

—Loss is temporary. God will restore you—

OMG! Operating as a Millennial with God

Reflection Questions

How do you handle loss?

_____

_____

_____

What Scriptures encourage you in difficult times?

_____

_____

_____

_____

_____

_____

_____

_____

_____

_____

_____

"God is still a God of restoration and healing. No situation is too far gone for God to restore."
— Brian Logue

Losing Friends

Friends come and go. Having fun is great, but having godly friends who support you, correct you and pray for you is priceless. Since relationships go both ways, you have to give as much as you receive. As you focus on being a godly, selfless friend, you'll experience closer, more-fulfilling relationships.

Friends come for a reason, a season or a lifetime. Losing friends is hurtful. It could be that they have completed their role in your life, so God isolated you. Not everyone is meant to stay with you. Ask God to send the friends He has for you. In the meantime, be at peace. Know that it's okay to let people go no matter how much history you have invested. When God closes a door, it's never to hurt you, but to push you toward His perfect will.

> *My friends are scoffers [who ridicule]; my eye pours out tears to God. Oh, that a man would mediate and plead with God [for me]. Just as a man [mediates and pleads] with his neighbor and friend.*
> —Job 16:20-21

> *A friend loves at all times, and a brother is born for a time of adversity.*
> —Proverbs 17:17 NKJV

Skylarr-Nicole Marsh

A man who has friends must himself be friendly, But there is a friend who sticks closer than a brother.
—Proverbs 18:24 NKJV

God, thank You for setting the example of godly friendships. Send friends who love You and operate with integrity. In my waiting, show me how to be the friend that You have called me to be. Let me be Your example. And when I feel like I have no one else, I know that I always have a friend in You. In Jesus' name, amen.

—Friends come and go,
but the ones who are
meant to stay will always be there—

OMG! Operating as a Millennial with God

Reflection Questions

How do you handle the loss of a friend?

_____

_____

_____

Have you asked God who He wants you to have as friends? Why or why not?

_____

_____

_____

What Scriptures illustrate qualities of genuine friends?

_____

_____

_____

_____

_____

_____

_____

Blessed are those who believe without seeing.
—John 20:29

OMG! Operating as a Millennial with God

Struggles in School

Whether exams, peer pressure or exclusion from team activities, the struggle for many students is real. The Bible teaches how to effectively overcome struggles: His Word. God is in control, so don't dwell on your failures, mistakes or circumstances. Whether you earn a 2.0 or 4.0, be faithful to your academic calling. When you feel like you don't measure up (whatever that means for you), ask God for help. He will increase your understanding and ability to recall information. Don't quit when you feel defeated. Your win is just around the corner.

As for these four young men, God gave them knowledge and skill in all kinds of literature and wisdom; Daniel also understood all kinds of visions and dreams.
—Daniel 1:17

Wisdom is the principal thing; therefore get wisdom. And in all your getting, get understanding.
—Proverbs 4:7

The mind of the prudent [always] acquires knowledge, and the ear of the wise [always] seeks knowledge.
—Proverbs 18:15

Skylarr-Nicole Marsh

God, thank You for giving me wisdom and understanding to get through school. Open my mind to learn and my ears to hear wisdom. Grant me total recall. Teach me how to teach others Your truth. Trials and hardships build me into a better person, when I yield complete control of my life, dreams and destiny to You. In Jesus' name, amen.

—Your schoolwork doesn't define you.
God has given you wisdom in all areas—

If any of you lacks wisdom [to guide him through a decision or circumstance], he is to ask of [our benevolent] God, who gives to everyone generously and without rebuke or blame, and it will be given to him.
—James 1:5

OMG! Operating as a Millennial with God

Reflection Questions

When you feel overwhelmed with school and all its responsibilities, how do you handle it?

_____

_____

_____

How can you apply prayer to that struggle?

_____

_____

_____

How do you work through peer pressure?

_____

_____

_____

Have you ever been the target of a bully? How did you deal with the situation?

_____

_____

_____

Skylarr-Nicole Marsh

What Scriptures help you move from victim to victor?

___

OMG! Operating as a Millennial with God

Struggling to Pray

Do you struggle to pray and seek God? Whether you don't know what to say, feel like God doesn't answer your prayers or have a hard time opening up, prayer is simply a conversation with God. Even if you feel like He doesn't hear or answer you, keep praying. You can talk to Him about anything, anywhere, anytime and in any way. You don't have to worry about Him using your words against you.

Like any conversation, listening is critical. Take time to listen for an answer. It can come directly from God, through His Word, a song, friend or stranger.

Although you may not receive an immediate response, know that delay is not denial. Many reasons can explain why your prayers aren't answered:
- Your request is not in your best interest
- Your request is contrary to His will
- You asked for the wrong reasons (James 4:3)
- Spiritual warfare delayed the response (Daniel 10:12-13)

Prayer changes the way you look at things, and when you go to God with a quiet soul, you'll be able to hear His answer. Never stop believing. Never stop trusting. Never stop praying.

Rejoice always and delight in your faith; be unceasing and persistent in prayer; in every situation [no matter what the circumstances] be thankful and continually give thanks to God; for this is the will of God for you in Christ Jesus.
—1 Thessalonians 5:16-18

Therefore, confess your sins to one another [your false steps, your offenses], and pray for one another, that you may be healed and restored. The heartfelt and persistent prayer of a righteous man (believer) can accomplish much [when put into action and made effective by God – it is dynamic and can have tremendous power].
—James 5:16

This is the [remarkable degree of] confidence which we [as believers are entitled to] have before Him: that if we ask anything according to His will, [consistent with His plan and purpose] He hears us.
—1 John 5:14

    Dear God, thank You for allowing me direct access to You through prayer. Even when it is hard for me to pray, I know my strength and confidence comes from You. My prayers won't be like anyone else's, but You hear me and You know me. I will always seek You because everything I need is in You. In Jesus' name, amen.

OMG! Operating as a Millennial with God

—Pray and pray again—

Reflections of My Heart
Praying has always been hard for me. I started with, "Dear God, thank You for this day," and then went into my list of thankfulness. I felt like my prayers were not being answered fast enough, but I pressed through and prayed. Don't let the enemy, friends or family tell you that God doesn't hear you. He does.

Rejoice always; pray without ceasing.
—1 Thessalonians 5:16-17

I found the perfect example of praying through the pain in the first six chapters of Psalms; specifically Psalm 6:6-10. In summary, David cried out to the Lord grieved. He commanded his enemies and workers of iniquity to depart from him. He trusted that the Lord heard his cry and received his prayer. Don't stop praying because God hears your prayers.

Reflection Questions

Do you find it hard to pray? Why or why not?

_____

_____

_____

How do you feel after you pray?

_____

_____

_____

When you have a hard time connecting to God in prayer, what Scriptures help you move closer to Him?

_____

_____

_____

_____

_____

_____

_____

In Christ

"Embrace uncertainty. Some of the most beautiful chapters in our lives won't have a title until much later."
— Bob Goff

OMG! Operating as a Millennial with God

God Wants You, Not Your Plans

Have you ever planned something with the greatest care and attention to detail, only to have a situation disrupt everything? Maybe you chose the perfect school for your major, accepted a great job or came into some unexpected money. You are living "the dream," and then a shift happens.

Situations can make you feel like God is taking away your dream for His calling. Just because it's a good thing, does not mean it's a God thing. He is gentle and loving. He will not force you, but rather nudge you in the right direction. It's not punishment. God loves you. He will never lead you astray. It may not be what you want, but obedience to God is more important.

> *"For I know the plans and thoughts that I have for you,"* says the Lord, *"plans for peace and well-being and not for disaster, to give you a future and a hope."*
> —Jeremiah 29:11

Recite this Scripture replacing the blanks with your name:

"For I know the plans and thoughts that I have for _____," says the Lord, *"plans for peace and well-being and not for disaster, to give _____ a future and a hope."*

Skylarr-Nicole Marsh

God, help me walk in Your will. I want to do one thing, but You are calling me to something greater than what my eyes can see. I trust You with the plans for my life. You never make mistakes. Everything is done in Your timing and in Your way. Let Your joy be my strength so I stay focused on You. In Jesus' name, amen.

—God knows what's best for you.
Trust Him with your life—

OMG! Operating as a Millennial with God

Reflection Questions

Do your dreams and desires match what God wants you to do? Why or why not?

_____

_____

_____

According to Psalm 37:4, if you delight yourself in the Lord, He will give you the desires of your heart. What are your desires? How do they line up with God's will for you?

_____

_____

_____

What other Scriptures define God's plan for you?

_____

_____

_____

_____

_____

_____

"We don't set the pace. It is God's plan, God's path, God's timing."
—Tim Hiller

OMG! Operating as a Millennial with God

The Promises of God

For all the promises of God in Him are yea, and in Him amen, unto the glory of God by us.
—2 Corinthians 1:20

God agrees with Himself (yea) and your obedience to His promises (amen). Throughout the Bible, God promised love, protection, new mercies, rest, victory, peace, provision, joy and much more. He established generational covenants with Abraham (Genesis 12:1-3) and David (2 Samuel 7:4-16) that are applicable to you. Like a child who reminds their parent of a promise, Gods wants you to speak His promises to Him and prove Him at His Word (Matthew 7:7-12).

Study Psalm 91, which describes the blessings of dwelling in His presence. These Scriptures represent a small portion of His promises:

Then it shall come about, because you listen to these judgments and keep and do them, that the Lord your God will keep with you the covenant and the [steadfast] lovingkindness which He swore to your fathers.
—Deuteronomy 7:12

It is the Lord who goes before you; He will be with you. He will not fail you or abandon you. Do not fear or be dismayed.
—Deuteronomy 31:8

If My people who are called by My name will humble themselves, and pray and seek My face, and turn from their wicked ways, then I will hear from heaven, and will forgive their sin and heal their land.
—2 Chronicles 7:14

The words and promises of the Lord are pure words, like silver refined in an earthen furnace, purified seven times.
—Psalm 12:6

Such hope [in God's promises] never disappoints [us] because God's love has been abundantly poured out within our hearts through the Holy Spirit who was given to us.
—Romans 5:5

OMG! Operating as a Millennial with God

Lord, I know that Your promises to me are true. Thank You for keeping Your Word. Titus 1:2 says that You cannot lie. Not that You choose not to lie, but You do not have the ability to lie. So, I trust that You will do exactly what You said. Help me walk in a "yes" and "amen" spirit. In Jesus' name, amen.

—Stand on the promises of God.
He will do exactly what He said—

Skylarr-Nicole Marsh

Reflection Questions

List God's promises and corresponding Scriptures.

_____

_____

_____

What things has God personally promised you?

_____

_____

_____

Even when you don't understand your life, do you still trust His promises?

_____

_____

_____

What Scriptures illustrate God's promises?

_____

_____

_____

_____

God's Strength

No matter how hard life gets, God's strength is perfect. It's important to learn how to rest in His power because He will take care of you. Since the power of life and death is in your tongue (Proverbs 18:21), know Scripture so you can speak the Word of God to change your life. "His strength is sufficient for me. God is always with me. The joy of the Lord is my strength." Quit trying to carry your burdens. He doesn't need your help. He wants your heart and trust. Ask Him to show up for you. Rest in His perfect strength and let Him carry you to victory.

"Do not sorrow, for the joy of the Lord is your strength."
—Nehemiah 8:10b

He gives strength to the weary, and to him who has no might He increases power.
— Isaiah 40:29

"But He has said to me, "My grace is sufficient for you [My lovingkindness and My mercy are more than enough — always available — regardless of the situation]; for [My] power is being perfected [and is completed and shows itself most effectively] in [your] weakness." Therefore, I will all the more gladly boast in my weaknesses, so that

the power of Christ [may completely enfold me and] may dwell in me. So I am well pleased with weaknesses, with insults, with distresses, with persecutions, and with difficulties, for the sake of Christ; for when I am weak [in human strength], then I am strong [truly able, truly powerful, truly drawing from God's strength]."
—2 Corinthians 12:9-10

After you have suffered for a little while, the God of all grace [who imparts His blessing and favor], who called you to His own eternal glory in Christ, will Himself complete, confirm, strengthen, and establish you [making you what you ought to be].
—1 Peter 5:10

Dear God, thank You for being my strength in times of weakness. I know that when I set my hope in You, You will strengthen and raise me at the appointed time. Thank You for placing Your Word in me. I will always find rest in You. In Jesus' name, amen.

—Let the joy of the Lord be your strength—

OMG! Operating as a Millennial with God

Reflection Questions

To whom or what do you turn, when you need strength?

_____

_____

_____

God's strength is perfect when yours is gone. Do you trust that He will carry you? Why or why not?

_____

_____

_____

What Scriptures define His omnipotent strength?

_____

_____

_____

_____

_____

_____

_____

"We aren't called to walk in our strength; we are called to walk in His."
— HeartPrintsOfGod.com

God's Timing

Waiting on God and trusting His timing are not the easiest things to do. Like the Children of Israel, becoming impatient and begging God for things that are not good for you can throw you out of God's timing and into mess. The excellence of His works is best when you wait on Him. Delay is not denial, so don't mistake God's timing for His absence.

Ecclesiastes 3:1-10 summarizes God's timing. A time to be born; a time to die. A time to plant; a time to pluck. A time to kill; a time to heal. A time to weep; a time to laugh. A time to rend; a time to sew. A time to keep silent; a time to speak. A time to love; a time to hate.

Trust the process. God is immortal and does not operate in finite time. A thousand years to us is like a day to Him (2 Peter 3:8).

> *He has made everything beautiful and appropriate in its time. He has also planted eternity [a sense of divine purpose] in the human heart [a mysterious longing which nothing under the sun can satisfy, except God] — yet man cannot find out (comprehend, grasp) what God has done (His overall plan) from the beginning to the end.*
> —Ecclesiastes 3:11

Skylarr-Nicole Marsh

Lord, thank You for making everything perfect in Your timing. Help me walk in Your will and plan for my life. Please order my steps, my life and the timing for everything. In Jesus' name, amen.

— Trust God. He never misses a beat and
He is always on time —

OMG! Operating as a Millennial with God

Reflection Questions

Read 1 Samuel 8. What happened to the Children of Israel when they begged God for a king to rule over them?

_____

_____

_____

Have you felt like you missed an opportunity?

_____

_____

_____

What did you *think* you missed?

_____

_____

_____

Was it as bad as you expected? Explain.

_____

_____

_____

What did God do instead?

_____

_____

_____

What other Scriptures describe God's infinite timing?

_____

_____

_____

_____

_____

_____

_____

_____

_____

_____

_____

_____

_____

_____

_____

Forgiveness

Forgiving someone, including yourself, is hard. Learning how to forgive and release painful, hurtful moments will help you move on, have peace and draw closer to God. Instead of being mad or hurt, give it to God, pray for peace and trust Him. Forgiveness is a marathon, not a sprint. The enemy will try to make you feel like you're alone, but you're not.

> *Let all bitterness, and wrath, and anger, and clamor, and evil speaking, be put away…and be kind to one another, tenderhearted, forgiving one another, even as God for Christ's sake has forgiven you.*
> —Ephesians 4:31-32

Don't let the enemy keep you bound by unforgiveness and bitterness. To live in peace and abundance, you must forgive.

> *Therefore there is now no condemnation [no guilty verdict, no punishment] for those who are in Christ Jesus [who believe in Him as personal Lord and Savior].*

For the law of the Spirit of life [which is] in Christ Jesus [the law of our new being] has set you free from the law of sin and of death.
—Romans 8:1-2

For if you forgive others their trespasses [their reckless and willful sins], your heavenly Father will also forgive you.
—Matthew 6:14

Dear God, thank You for dying on the cross. Thank You for forgiving my sins. That reason alone is why I should freely forgive, but it's hard. Create in me a clean heart to receive your forgiveness and extend forgiveness to others. Thank You for being there every step of the way. In Jesus' name, amen.

—Forgive to be forgiven—

OMG! Operating as a Millennial with God

Reflection Questions

How does unforgiveness affect you?

_____

_____

_____

What Scriptures illustrate the power forgiveness?

_____

_____

_____

Reflection Activity

Create a forgiveness prayer that you recite aloud daily as follows:
- Thank God for forgiving you of your sins and placing them into the sea of forgetfulness.
- List things for which you have not forgiven others. Speak each person's name, the offense and then ask God to move you to a state of forgiveness. Release the person from your head and heart to God's greater good.
- List things done to others for which you have not forgiven yourself. Ask God to move you to a state of forgiveness. Release yourself to God's greater good.
- List things done to yourself for which you have not forgiven yourself. Ask God to move you to a state of forgiveness. Release yourself to God's greater good.

_____

_____

_____

_____

_____

_____

_____

OMG! Operating as a Millennial with God

Skylarr-Nicole Marsh

Calling on Jesus

I often joke with my friends and say, "You better call on Jesus, not me." Although I say that to be funny, the statement is true. When a situation comes, are you quick to run to the phone or the throne?

The name of Jesus is powerful. Strongholds break, sickness leaves, situations change and demons are subject to His name. His Word is true and will never return void. He promised to supply your needs, love you, fight your battles, order your steps and keep you safe in His arms.

I do not want to put the responsibly of my protection, peace and provision on a friend; that's God's job! Friends and family have limits and limited resources, but God is limitless. That's why it is important to call Jesus. Get to know Him, develop a relationship and learn how to pray. He is waiting for you to speak the Word and activate your faith. He will be there every time you call.

I sought the Lord, and He heard me, and delivered me from all my fears.
—Psalm 34:4 NKJV

For this reason also [because He obeyed and so completely humbled Himself], God has highly exalted Him and bestowed on Him the name which is above every name, so that at the name of

Jesus every knee shall bow [in submission], of those who are in heaven and on earth and under the earth, and that every tongue will confess and openly acknowledge that Jesus Christ is Lord (sovereign God), to the glory of God the Father.
—Philippians 2:9-11

Therefore, since we are surrounded by so great a cloud of witnesses [who by faith have testified to the truth of God's absolute faithfulness], stripping off every unnecessary weight and the sin which so easily and cleverly entangles us, let us run with endurance and active persistence the race that is set before us, [looking away from all that will distract us and] focusing our eyes on Jesus, who is the Author and Perfecter of faith [the first incentive for our belief and the One who brings our faith to maturity], who for the joy [of accomplishing the goal] set before Him endured the cross, disregarding the shame, and sat down at the right hand of the throne of God [revealing His deity, His authority, and the completion of His work].
—Hebrews 12:1-2

Dear God, Your Son, Jesus, is great. When I feel the need to call somebody, I call You...any time! Thank You for being there when others aren't. Thank You for drawing me under Your wings. Although I am one of billions who need You, Your love is so great. You know my troubles, my concerns and You

OMG! Operating as a Millennial with God

care about my dreams. I am blessed to be able to call You whenever and wherever I need. In You, I have peace, joy, safety and love. In Jesus' name, amen.

—Jesus, Jesus, Jesus; at the mention of Your name—

Reflection Questions

How do you feel when you call on Jesus?

What situations changed, when you said His name?

What Scriptures illustrate how Jesus shows up when you call Him?

OMG! Operating as a Millennial with God

The Beauty in Being You

As sure as you breathe, someone will talk about you. Whether social media, family, classmates or co-workers, people will say and do things to try to change you, make you feel bad or cause others to dislike you. Never let that faze you. God made you who you are.

> *I praise You because I am fearfully and wonderfully made; Your works are wonderful, I know that full well.*
> —Psalm 139:14

You are the best at being you, so don't try to be anyone else. Be firm in your spiritual and personal beliefs; not swayed by crowds or popular opinion. Approximately 25% of the people you meet love you; 25% dislike you and 50% are indifferent. Focus on the top 25% who love you and put your confidence in God.

> *"Before I formed you in the womb I knew you; Before you were born I sanctified you; I ordained you a prophet to the nations."*
> —Jeremiah 1:5 NKJV

Skylarr-Nicole Marsh

Blessed [with spiritual security] is the man who believes and trusts in and relies on the Lord, and whose hope and confident expectation is the Lord.
—Jeremiah 17:7

In whom we have boldness and confident access through faith in Him [that is, our faith gives us sufficient courage to freely and openly approach God through Christ]."
—Ephesians 3:12

Dear God, thank You for creating me the way You saw fit. Pressure from family, friends and social media will try to change me, but I am confident in who I am in You. With freedom and confidence, I can be myself when I approach You. Thank You for looking beyond my faults and loving me. Thank You for doing a great work in me. In Jesus' name, amen.

—GODfidence: the confidence that
God placed inside you—

OMG! Operating as a Millennial with God

Reflection Questions

Is it easy for you to find your true confidence in Christ? Why or why not?

_____

_____

_____

What Scriptures define how God sees you?

_____

_____

_____

_____

_____

_____

_____

_____

_____

_____

_____

Skylarr-Nicole Marsh

"I found I was more confident when I stopped trying to be someone else's definition of beautiful and started being my own."
— Remington Miller

OMG! Operating as a Millennial with God
A Better Relationship with God

A relationship with God is the best relationship you can have. When you accept Him as your Lord and Savior, He comes into your heart and His Spirit reunites with yours. Verbal confession and sincere belief that God raised Jesus from the dead are all you need to be saved.

Your spiritual relationship sets the tone for every other relationship. Don't look to man for needs that only God can fill. When you seek Him, powerful things happen: fear leaves, compassion arrives and you focus on what God is doing in and through you.

> *Because if you acknowledge and confess with your mouth that Jesus is Lord [recognizing His power, authority and majesty as God], and believe in your heart that God raised Him from the dead, you will be saved. For with the heart a person believes [in Christ as Savior] resulting in his justification [that is, being made righteous — being freed of the guilt of sin and made acceptable to God]; and with the mouth he acknowledges and confesses [his faith openly], resulting in and confirming [his] salvation.*
> —Romans 10:9-10

Therefore as you have received Christ Jesus the Lord, walk in [union with] Him [reflecting His

character in the things you do and say — living lives that lead others away from sin], having been deeply rooted [in Him] and now being continually built up in Him and [becoming increasingly more] established in your faith, just as you were taught, and overflowing in it with gratitude.
—Colossians 2:6-7

God, I don't always make time to seek Your presence. I know You are always with me, even when I back away from You. Let Your spirit and Word inspire me to become like You. Thank You for overwhelming me with Your love, grace and mercy. I will always praise You. I will always be alive in You. In Jesus' name, amen.

—God will never leave or forsake you.
He is always near, even when you think He's far—

OMG! Operating as a Millennial with God

Reflection Questions

What is the status of your relationship with God?

_____

_____

_____

If it's not where you want it to be, what can you do to change it?

_____

_____

_____

What Scriptures demonstrate God's desire to have a relationship with you?

_____

_____

_____

_____

_____

_____

_____

"God promised to never leave you, so if you're feeling disconnected from Him, understand that you changed; not Him."
—Skylarr Marsh

OMG! Operating as a Millennial with God

Finding Your Identity in Christ

Have you tried to find yourself in other people or things? In most cases, you're still not satisfied because worldly things cannot fill a spiritual void.

Find your identity in Christ. He knows you, your preferences, strengths and weaknesses. He is the only one from whom you need validation. Since you are created in His image and likeness, don't let social media, friends or family define you; especially if it's negative. Spend time with Him—reading, praying and living the Word—and you'll find yourself in the process. Roadblocks will come to bring you low, but speak 2 Corinthians 5:17 out loud and trust God.

When you speak the Scripture, replace the blanks with your name:

Therefore, if _____ is in Christ, _____ is a new creation; old things have passed away; behold, all things have become new.
—2 Corinthians 5:17

So God created man in His own image, in the image and likeness of God He created him; male and female He created them.
—Genesis 1:27

"Before I formed you in the womb I knew you; before you were born I sanctified you; I ordained you a prophet to the nations."
—Jeremiah 1:5

But you are a chosen race, a royal priesthood, a consecrated nation, a [special] people for God's own possession, so that you may proclaim the excellences [the wonderful deeds and virtues and perfections] of Him who called you out of darkness into His marvelous light.
—1 Peter 2:9

Dear God, thank You for letting me see myself as You see me. I don't have to search worldly things to find my identity. I am created in Your image and nobody can take that from me. Help me help others identify themselves in You. In Jesus' name, amen.

—God created you the way He saw fit.
Be confident in that—

OMG! Operating as a Millennial with God

Reflection Questions

What things do you view about yourself that God sees differently?

_____

_____

_____

What Scriptures speak to your identity in Christ?

_____

_____

_____

_____

_____

_____

_____

_____

_____

_____

_____

"Don't seek validation from people and things. Reflect on what God says about you: fearfully and wonderfully made, created in His image and filled with His Spirit. Think on those things that are good, pure, lovely, honest and just (Philippians 4:8)."
—Skylarr Marsh

OMG! Operating as a Millennial with God
Speak God's Word over Your Life

Many problems are directly related to the choices you make. Other than family, you choose most of the people in your life. You choose to let your emotions—depression, anxiety, stress, fear—dictate your actions. You choose your esteem; whether low or high. Instead of fussing, crying and complaining, speak the Word! Confess your greatness in Him. The Word of God is powerful.

> *For the Word of God is living and active and full of power [making it operative, energizing, and effective]. It is sharper than any two-edged sword, penetrating as far as the division of the soul and spirit [the completeness of a person], and of both joints and marrow [the deepest parts of our nature], exposing and judging the very thoughts and intentions of the heart.*
> —Hebrews 4:12

God did not promise a life without challenges, but He did promise to always provide you with an escape plan (I Corinthians 10:13). When you feel anxious, recite Philippians 4:6-7. When you need comfort, read Matthew 5:4. Are you struggling with depression? Read Psalm 40:1-3. When you need guidance, study Psalm 32:8. Do you need healing? Read Isaiah 53:5 and I Peter 2:21-25. These Scripture are just a few of the many references that help you speak life to your issues. The Lord will fight your battles if you keep still. Keep applying the Word and watch things change.

Let the [spoken] Word of Christ have its home within you [dwelling in your heart and mind — permeating every aspect of your being] as you teach [spiritual things] and admonish and train one another with all wisdom, singing psalms and hymns and spiritual songs with thankfulness in your hearts to God. Whatever you do [no matter what it is] in word or deed, do everything in the name of the Lord Jesus [and in dependence on Him], giving thanks to God the Father through Him.
—Colossians 3:16-17

But as for you, continue in the things that you have learned and of which you are convinced [holding tightly to the truths], knowing from whom you learned them, and how from childhood you have known the sacred writings which are able to give you the wisdom that leads to salvation through faith which is in Christ Jesus [surrendering your entire self to Him and having absolute confidence in His wisdom, power and goodness]. All Scripture is God-breathed [given by divine inspiration] and is profitable for instruction, for conviction [of sin], for correction [of error and restoration to obedience], for

OMG! Operating as a Millennial with God

training in righteousness [learning to live in conformity to God's will, both publicly and privately — behaving honorably with personal integrity and moral courage]; so that the man of God may be complete and proficient, outfitted and thoroughly equipped for every good work.
—2 Timothy 3:14-17

Dear God, thank You for sending Your Word so I can have Your perfect instructions on how to live the life You created for me. When I feel overwhelmed, I go to Your Word and find everything I need. Help me apply the Word to my life, so I can effectively walk upright before You. In Jesus' name, amen.

— Anybody can fist fight, but do you know how to fight in the Spirit? —

Reflection Questions

What battles do you fight instead of letting God fight for you?

_____

_____

_____

How has operating in your strength worked for you?

_____

_____

_____

When you feel overwhelmed, what Scriptures help you solve your problems?

_____

_____

_____

What prayers do you say?

_____

_____

_____

OMG! Operating as a Millennial with God

What Scriptures encourage you to speak things into existence?

_____

_____

_____

Make a list of "I am" statements. For example, I am blessed. I am beautiful. I am gifted. I am fearfully and wonderfully made. Recite these affirmations aloud, twice a day.

_____

_____

_____

_____

_____

_____

_____

_____

_____

_____

Living for Christ

Life can be difficult, so why not live for Christ? Because God's standards are higher than man's, you can't always do what your friends do, or like me, you may not fit in with peers. Guess what. It's okay to not be part of the crowd. You don't have to be "young and dumb." You can be young, have fun and filled with the Holy Spirit.

Going to church, praying, reading your Bible and sharing God's goodness is not shameful, despite what others may believe. If someone wants you to compromise your love for Christ, then they are not right for you. Young people attract other young people; so as you speak about your love for Christ, you can draw others to Him. Don't let pressure or rejection silence you. Stand for Christ, so He can stand in you.

And I, if and when I am lifted up from the earth [on the cross], will draw all people to Myself [Gentiles, as well as Jews]."
—John 12:32

I am not ashamed of the gospel, for it is the power of God for salvation [from His wrath and punishment] to everyone who believes [in Christ as Savior], to the Jew first and also to the Greek.
—Romans 1:16

For we are His workmanship [His own master work, a work of art], created in Christ Jesus [reborn from above — spiritually transformed, renewed, ready to be used] for good works, which God prepared [for us] beforehand [taking paths which He set], so that we would walk in them [living the good life which He prearranged and made ready for us].
—Ephesians 2:10

Dear God, thank You for giving me Your Spirit. Shine through me so Christ can overflow onto others. Teach me to live boldly for You. Help my generation live righteously, be different from the world and be a light to others. In Jesus' name, amen.

—Live for Christ even when you don't fit in with those around you—

OMG! Operating as a Millennial with God

Reflection Questions

Will you live boldly for Christ even when others don't?

_____

_____

_____

What does 1 Peter 4:4-11 mean to you?

_____

_____

_____

What other Scriptures illustrate living for Christ?

_____

_____

_____

_____

_____

_____

_____

_____

"Living for Christ may sometimes make you feel ignored, rejected and talked about, but God will be there through every hurt, pain and disappointment."
—Skylarr Marsh

Faith

What does faith mean to you? In whom—or what—do you have faith?

Faith is when you can't see something, but you believe it's there. For example, have you ever played the game where you stand in front of someone, then fall backwards? Because you have faith in your friend, you surrender your safety to their ability to catch you. With faith in God, you surrender your plans and will to Him.

How has God shown His faithfulness to you? Obstacles can cause you to lose faith in God. And when you do not understand why it seems like nothing works for you, your faith can fail quickly.

Have you ever looked at others' lives and questioned God about yours? Put your faith and trust in God. Mustard-seed faith moves mountains. Things may not be working for you at this moment, but if you put your faith in Him, He will do exactly what He said He will do. Without faith it is impossible to please God, so when you go to Him with a need, believe that He will provide. His provision may not come how or when you want, but if it's His will for you, it will be done. God rewards those who diligently seek Him (Hebrews 11:6).

> He answered, "Because of your little faith [your lack of trust and confidence in the power of God];

for I assure you and most solemnly say to you, if you have [living] faith the size of a mustard seed, you will say to this mountain, 'Move from here to there,' and [if it is God's will] it will move; and nothing will be impossible for you."
—Matthew 17:20

Now faith is the assurance (title deed, confirmation) of things hoped for (divinely guaranteed), and the evidence of things not seen [the conviction of their reality—faith comprehends as fact what cannot be experienced by the physical senses].
—Hebrews 11:1

Dear God, help my faith. Help me put my problems, worries and issues in Your hands and leave them there. Even when I fear and doubt, You have already made a way. Fear does nothing for me, but faith activates You to move mountains, break chains, reveal opportunities and revive my family. In Jesus' name, amen.

—Your faith can move mountains—

OMG! Operating as a Millennial with God

Reflection Questions

What is faith to you?

_____

_____

_____

How can you apply faith to your situations?

_____

_____

_____

List your favorite faith Scriptures.

_____

_____

_____

_____

_____

_____

_____

"The principal part of faith is patience. Knowing that God has your best intentions in mind, ask Him to give you power to stand while you wait on Him."
—Skylarr Marsh

OMG! Operating as a Millennial with God

Trusting God

Trust is putting action to your faith. Using the example in the previous lesson, you believe your friend has the **ability** to catch you, but do you trust him/her enough to let go? How many times did you attempt to fall, only to catch yourself?

Per Webster.com, trust is "firm belief in the reliability, truth, ability, or strength of someone or something." The way you trust God, is not the same way you trust man. Family, friends and loved ones can intentionally or unintentionally cause you to fail; and they often make promises they can't keep. God isn't like that. When you read His Word and pray, you begin to trust Him. He backs up His promises. He will catch you when you fall.

> *And those who know Your name [who have experienced Your precious mercy] will put their confident trust in You, for You, O Lord, have not abandoned those who seek You.*
> —Psalm 9:10
>
> *When I am afraid, I will put my trust and faith in You.*
> —Psalm 56:3

Skylarr-Nicole Marsh

Trust in and rely confidently on the Lord with all your heart. And do not rely on your own insight or understanding.

In all your ways know, acknowledge and recognize Him, and He will make your paths straight and smooth [removing obstacles that block your way].
—Proverbs 3:5-6

    Lord Jesus, I know that You did not create me to worry or fear. Your Word says that You will never leave me lonely. I put my trust in You. You have never failed me, and You never will. Thank You for sending Your Word and Your Spirit to help me, especially when I can't see You working in my life. In Jesus' name, amen.

—Put your faith in God.
Trust Him in every area of your life—

OMG! Operating as a Millennial with God

Reflection Questions

What does trust mean to you?

_____

_____

_____

What things make it hard for you to trust God?

_____

_____

_____

How do you plan to trust Him in all things?

_____

_____

_____

What Scriptures encourage you to trust God?

_____

_____

_____

_____

_____

"I can rest in the fact that God is in control, which means I can face things that are out of my control and not act out of control."
—Lysa Terkeurst

OMG! Operating as a Millennial with God

Pursuing Peace

With all the chaos in the world, pursuing peace as a lifestyle should be your focus. God never intended for you to live in chaos. Life disruptions may put you there for a while, but He does not want you to take residence in it.

Worldly peace is temporary. Possessions, places, people and self-medication are "quick fixes" for problems. However, when you have a relationship with Christ and study His Word, peace is not hard to find. Godly peace offers rest and assurance that He will take care of you. He is Jehovah Shalom, the Prince of Peace. When attacks make you feel like you're out of control or losing your mind, speak God's Word back to Him.

In Mark 4:25-31, Jesus calmed raging waters, rebuked winds and spoke to the storm, "Peace, be still." Guess what. The storm ceased! You have that same authority. Rename your storm from chaos to peace, command the turbulence to stop and trust God to honor His promise.

The Lord will give [unyielding and impenetrable] strength to His people; The Lord will bless His people with peace.
—Psalm 29:11

Skylarr-Nicole Marsh

Peace I leave with you; My [perfect] peace I give to you; not as the world gives do I give to you. Do not let your heart be troubled, nor let it be afraid. [Let My perfect peace calm you in every circumstance and give you courage and strength for every challenge.]
—John 14:27

Be anxious for nothing, but in everything by prayer and supplication, with thanksgiving, let your requests be made known to God; and the peace of God, which surpasses all understanding, will guard your hearts and minds through Christ Jesus.
—Philippians 4:6-7

Dear God, thank You for giving me Your peace; peace far beyond my understanding. Everything I need, I can find in You. Thank You for being my peace, strength and shelter in times of storm. Peace is my portion, and I thank You for giving it to me. In Jesus' name, amen.

—Ask God for peace that
surpasses all understanding—

OMG! Operating as a Millennial with God

Reflection Questions

What situations steal your peace?

_____

_____

_____

How will your perspective change knowing the peace God will give you?

_____

_____

_____

What Scriptures provide you with peace?

_____

_____

_____

_____

_____

_____

_____

_____

Skylarr-Nicole Marsh

God is not man, that He should lie, or a son of man, that He should change His mind. Has He said, and will He not do it? Or has He spoken, and will He not fulfill it?
—Numbers 23:19

Spiritual Reference

The Lord is near to all who call on Him, to all who call on Him in truth. He fulfills the desires of those who fear Him; He hears their cry and saves them.
—Psalm 145:18-19

OMG! Operating as a Millennial with God

The Holy Spirit

The works of the Holy Spirit will lead you, as you live for Christ. He will be your teacher and produce many good fruits in your life.

So that the [righteous and just] requirement of the Law might be fulfilled in us who do not live our lives in the ways of the flesh [guided by worldliness and our sinful nature], but [live our lives] in the ways of the Spirit [guided by His power].
—Romans 8:4

The Holy Spirit is your teacher.
But the Helper (Comforter, Advocate, Intercessor — Counselor, Strengthener, Standby), the Holy Spirit, whom the Father will send in My name [in My place, to represent Me and act on My behalf], He will teach you all things. And He will help you remember everything that I have told you.
—John 14:26

The Holy Spirit will also help you produce fruit.
But the fruit of the Spirit [the result of His presence within us] is love [unselfish concern for others], joy, [inner] peace, patience [not the ability to wait, but how we act while waiting], kindness,

goodness, faithfulness, gentleness, self-control. Against such things there is no law.
—Galatians 5:22-23

In Him, you also, when you heard the word of truth, the good news of your salvation, and [as a result] believed in Him, were stamped with the seal of the promised Holy Spirit [the One promised by Christ] as owned and protected [by God]. The Spirit is the guarantee [the first installment, the pledge, a foretaste] of our inheritance until the redemption of God's own [purchased] possession [His believers], to the praise of His glory.
—Ephesians 1:13-14

And I will ask the Father, and He will give you another Helper (Comforter, Advocate, Intercessor — Counselor, Strengthener, Standby), to be with you forever — the Spirit of Truth, whom the world cannot receive [and take to its heart] because it does not see Him or know Him, but you know Him because He (the Holy Spirit) remains with you continually and will be in you.
—John 14:16-17

OMG! Operating as a Millennial with God

God, thank You for the Father, Son and Holy Spirit that lead, guide and protect me. Without You, I am incomplete. Thank You for being my present help, intercessor, comfort, joy and peace. Thank You, Holy Spirit, for being everything I need. In Jesus' name, amen.

—Let the Holy Spirit lead and guide you—

Skylarr-Nicole Marsh

Reflection Question

What Scriptures illustrate the purpose and power of the Holy Spirit?

Acknowledgements

I give all the glory, honor and praise to God. Lord, please be glorified in this project. Let Your light shine in me, so I can encourage others.

To my mother, Robin Marsh: Mom, thank you for everything. Words will never express how grateful I am for your guidance, support and prayers. I appreciate and love you!

My grandparents: Arthur and Shirley Walton; PopPop and Grandmother. Thank you for your unconditional love and support. You loved me like I needed, and I'm forever grateful. I miss you.

Grandma Johnnie, your guidance, prayers and support are priceless. Thank you for everything you do for me and for being the perfect example of "pushing through the pain."

To my brother, D'Juan Walton, my sister, LaDonna Walton, and my nieces, Taylor, Tiera, and Aalyee Walton: Thank you for always being there to support, encourage and push me to greater.

To my family: Thank you for years of support, prayers and encouragement. You have been there for me in many different ways.

To my pastor, Samuel N. Winston, Jr., Lady Chanel Winston and Mt. Calvary MBC family: Thank you for introducing me to Christ, and giving me godly advice that I can apply in my life. Because of you, I know God and how much He loves me.

To my sister-friends and POWER Team: Ta'Juana Page, Anarra Williams, Kyra Snowden, J'la Drummond, Jada Bolden, Yvonne Precious Plump, Valencia Woodard, Lashawn Ford, Courtni Jackson, Samera Black and India Foster. You are valuable to me in many ways. I am grateful for our "sister-ship" and love you forever. Thank you for your priceless feedback on the creation of *OMG!*

To my leading ladies: Shondale Dorise, Chantris Holly, Montina Berryhill, Harriet Watson, Cheryl Brooks, Kristal Corbitt, Tara Bolden, Rhine Phillips, Toyal Wortham, Beatrice Page, Deborah Berry, Marilyn Byrd-Rutledge, Charlene Hall, Jama Stephens, Shurnie Winston, Gwendolyn Clinkscales, Mayor Mary McDonald, Tina Toles, Natisha Hogan, Mo'nic Hogan, Shannon Dorsey, Inez Nunley, Onita Morgan-Edwards, Rolanda Mattison-Pruitt, Laura-Stewart Trayvick, LaTeasa Spears, Rhea Adkins Daria Dillard-Stone and many others. Thank you for imparting into me. Your help, advice and prayers helped shape me into the woman I am today. From the bottom of my heart, thank you.

To my mighty men of God: Clinton Yokely, Robert Berryhill, Thomas Rutledge, Jr., Willis 'Bing' Davis, Pastor Paul Gales and Kyran Snowden. Thank you for working with me, praying for me and leading me in a godly way.

Finally, to every person who ever prayed for me, believed in me, loved me and supported me; thank you.

About the Author

Compassionate. Thoughtful. Patient. Skylarr-Nicole Marsh has a servant's heart and helping hands. When she's not spending time with family, she's connecting with God or encouraging millennials by sharing godly solutions to worldly problems.

Having fulfilled her lifelong dream of being a published author, Skylarr aspires to be a nurse. She hopes to travel the world caring for people. She is active in church, and enjoys going to Sinclair College. Skyalrr plans to graduate in 2020 with an associate's degree in public health. She has volunteered with many organizations including House of Bread, YMCA and the Mustard Seed Foundation in service to her community.

In 2018, Skylarr launched Flourish and Grow, LLC—and its companion t-shirt line—as encouragement to be all God called you to be.

Email Skylarr at info@skylarrmarsh.com to share your experience with *OMG!* For inquiries about speaking engagements, bulk book purchases or t-shirt orders, visit SkylarrMarsh.com.

SkylarrMarsh.com

Skylarr-Nicole Marsh

OMG! Operating as a Millennial with God

About Queen V Publishing

The Doorway to YOUR Destiny!

Go thou and publish abroad the kingdom of God.

—Luke 9:60 ESV

Committed to transforming manuscripts into polished works of art, **Queen V Publishing** is a company of standard and integrity. We offer an alternative that allows the message in YOU to do what it was sent to do for OTHERS.

QueenVPublishing.com

Serving professional speakers and experts to magnify and monetize their message by publishing quality books

www.ingramcontent.com/pod-product-compliance
Lightning Source LLC
Chambersburg PA
CBHW050437010526
44118CB00013B/1570